Klett

10-Minuten-Training

Englisch Grammatik

# Simple Present und Present Progressive

5. Klasse

Kleine Lernportionen für jeden Tag

Peggy Fehily, Karin Kimmich, Andreas Kuhn, Petra Lihocky,
Sarah Nowotny, Alexander P. Saccaro, Dieter Vilimek

Klett Lerntraining

Bibliografische Information der Deutschen Nationalbibliothek
Die Deutsche Nationalbibliothek verzeichnet diese Publikation in der Deutschen Nationalbibliografie; detaillierte bibliografische Daten sind im Internet über http://dnb.dnb.de abrufbar.



1. Auflage 2017


www.klett-lerntraining.de

Umschlag: Sabine Kaufmann, Stuttgart
Umschlagfoto: www.thomas-weccard.de
Layout und Satz: tebitron gmbh, Gerlingen
Druck: medienhaus Plump GmbH, Rheinbreitbach
Printed in Germany
ISBN 978-3-12-927389-0

# Inhaltsverzeichnis

# Vorwort

Hallo!

Wie ist das bei dir: Blickst du bei *simple present* und *present progressive* auch nicht so richtig durch? Und du weißt gar nicht, wie du üben sollst?

Keine Sorge, diese beiden Zeiten kannst du super lernen! Unser Tipp: Lerne nicht alles an einem Tag. Übe lieber jeden Tag 10 Minuten!

Das geht superschnell und du übst trotzdem intensiver als sonst. Die kleine Uhr erinnert dich daran: besser kleine Lernportionen.

In diesem Heft sind über 70 Übungen zu den beiden Zeitformen. **Tipp**kästen helfen dir mit wichtigen Regeln weiter. Leichtere Übungen haben ein Sternchen ★☆ und etwas schwerere Übungen haben zwei Sternchen ★★. Fange am besten mit den leichteren Übungen an!

Wir wünschen dir viel Erfolg!

Deine Klett-Lerntraining-Redaktion

Immer nur 10 Minuten!

# 1 Simple present

## Die einfach Form der Gegenwart

**1** ★☆ **Welches Verb passt in die Lücke? Kreuze an.**

a) We ______________ in a small village. ☐ live ☐ like

b) I usually ______________ my bike to school. ☐ write ☐ ride

c) They ______________ in the city centre. ☐ work ☐ enjoy

d) You ______________ too fast! ☐ sing ☐ speak

e) I ______________ pizza. ☐ love ☐ live

f) We often ______________ computer games. ☐ play ☐ drive

g) Ben and Andy never ______________ shopping. ☐ have ☐ go

h) You ______________ a lot of TV. ☐ walk ☐ watch

**Tipp**

In folgenden Fällen benutzt du die einfache Gegenwart:
- wenn du über Gewohnheiten sprichst.
- wenn du über regelmäßige Ereignisse sprichst.
- wenn du über Handlungen, die aufeinander folgen, sprichst.

Die Verbformen im *simple present* haben nicht alle dieselbe Endung. Zum Glück musst du dir aber nur zwei Formen merken:
- Bei *I*, *you*, *we* und *they* hat das Verb dieselbe Form wie der Infinitiv.
- Nur bei Nomen in der 3. Person Singular und dementsprechend auch bei *he*, *she* und *it* musst du ein -s anhängen.

*I like orange juice.*
*We eat lots of cornflakes.*
*Patrick often drinks lemonade.*
*She plays the drums.*
*Our cat climbs trees at night.*

**2** ★☆ **Ein Tierrätsel! Setze die unten stehenden Verben im *simple present* in die Lücken ein. Nenne anschließend das Tier, um das es geht.**

work | carry | laugh | be | be | call | sound | live

a) I ____________________ a very big animal.

b) My voice ____________________ like a trumpet.

c) I ____________________ in Africa or in Asia.

d) The colour of my skin ____________________ grey.

e) You ____________________ my nose a "trunk".

f) I ____________________ heavy things or people on my back.

g) Some of my brothers and sisters ____________________ in circuses.

h) Silly people ____________________ about my ears.

**The name of the animal is** ____________________

**3** ★☆ **Trage die richtigen Verben in das Kreuzworträtsel ein.**

a) ________ a song

b) ________ shopping

c) ________ the time

d) ________ a glass of water

e) ________ a question

f) ________ a letter

g) ________ here

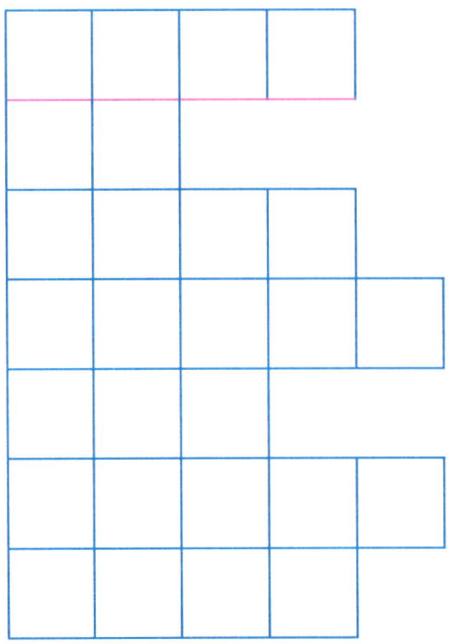

**4** ★☆ **Was tut Familie Benson am Abend? Übersetze die hervorgehobenen Signalwörter für das *simple present*.**

a) They **often** play with their children. ______________________

b) They **always** talk to them. ______________________

c) They **often** help them with their homework. ______________________

d) They **usually** watch TV or read a book. ______________________

e) They **sometimes** go out. ______________________

f) They **never** stay out all night. ______________________

g) **Sometimes** their friends come to see them. ______________________

h) They **always** have a good time. ______________________

i) They are **seldom** bored. ______________________

j) They **never** get angry. ______________________

**5** ★☆ **Sieh dir Aufgabe 4 nochmals an, und kreuze dann die richtigen Antworten an.**

a) Wo stehen die Signalwörter bei den einfachen Formen von to be?

☐ vor dem Verb ☐ hinter dem Verb

b) Wo stehen die Signalwörter bei dem simple present?

☐ vor dem Verb ☐ hinter dem Verb?

c) Wo stehen die Signalwörter bei verneinten Formen des simple present?

☐ vor dem Verb ☐ hinter dem Verb

d) Wo kann sometimes noch stehen?

☐ überall ☐ am Satzanfang

**6** ★☆ **Schreibe die Sätze in der richtigen Reihenfolge auf.**

a) She gets up.

b) She leaves the house.

c) She cleans her teeth.

d) Annie's alarm clock rings.

e) She catches the bus to school.

f) She wakes up.

g) She has breakfast.

Richtige Reihenfolge: _____ _____ _____ _____ _____ _____ _____

**Tipp**

So bildest du das *simple present:*

- In der dritten Person Singular wird im *simple present* immer ein -*s* angehängt.
- Wenn kein -*e* vorhanden ist, wird bei Verben, die auf einen Zischlaut enden (= -*ch*, -*ss*, -*sh*, -*x*, -*z*), ein -*es* angehängt: *watch* → *watches*.
- Bei Verben, die wie *to fly* auf Konsonant + *y* enden, wird das -*ys* zu -*ies*. *He flies home.*
- Bei Verben, die wie *to play* auf Vokal + *y* enden, ändert sich das -*y* nicht: *He plays at home.*

Besonderheiten:

*He goes home.*
*He does his homework.*
Bei *to go* und *to do* wird in der dritten Person Singular ein -*es* angehängt.

*He has breakfast.*
*He has a drink.*
Bedeutet *have* nicht „besitzen", so ist es ein Vollverb. Es steht dann immer ohne *got*.

**7** ★☆ **a) Setze die dritte Person Singular ein.**

he ________________________ (play) she ________________________ (do)

he ________________________ (carry) she ________________________ (watch)

she ________________________ (go) he ________________________ (die)

he ________________________ (say) she ________________________ (kiss)

he ________________________ (try) she ________________________ (have)

he ________________________ (buy) she ________________________ (make)

**b) Unterstreiche die Verben, die unregelmäßig sind, und schreibe sie heraus.**

________________________ ________________________

________________________ ________________________

**8** ★★ **Schreibe die Sätze neu und benutze die 3. Person Singular.**
**Denk daran – *he*, *she*, *it* – das *s* muss mit!**

a) I come from Frankfurt.

Jonas ____________________________________________

b) You never answer a question.

Marie ____________________________________________

c) We usually watch a film on Saturday evening.

Michael ____________________________________________

d) They send a lot of texts.

Caroline ____________________________________________

**9** ★★ **In der Wörterschlange unten stehen die Verben, die du für die Lücken benötigst. Markiere zunächst die Wortgrenzen. Die Verben stehen bereits in der richtigen Reihenfolge, aber im Infinitiv. Setze sie im *simple present* in die Lücken ein.**

behavegotturnsinggoneedcutheatputaddcookfeel

a) Mr Smith ____________________ a very good cook.

b) He ____________________ his own recipe (Rezept) for a spaghetti sauce.

c) First he ____________________ on the music.

d) He ____________________ an Italian song.

e) Then he ____________________ into the garden …

f) …because he ____________________ some basil (Basilikum).

g) Next he ____________________ an onion and some garlic into small pieces.

h) Then he ____________________ some oil in a frying pan (Pfanne).

i) He ____________________ the onion and the garlic into the hot oil.

j) After that he ____________________ a tin of tomatoes, salt, pepper and the basil.

k) Finally he ____________________ the spaghetti in a big pot.

l) Now he ____________________ ready for another Italian song.

**10** ★★ **Bringe die Wörter in die richtige Reihenfolge.**

**Beispiel:** work / they / hard / don't / very *They don't work very hard.*

a) don't / clothes / expensive / I / buy

___

b) night / birds / don't / at / sing

___

c) my / know / you / name / don't

___

d) watch / in / we / evening / TV / don't / the

___

e) swimming / don't / I / enjoy

___

f) Lucas / videos / and / watch / Sophie / don't

___

**Tipp**

Wenn du Aussagen in der einfachen Gegenwart verneinst, nimmst du *don't* und in der 3. Person Singular *doesn't*.

*I don't like sausages.*
*Joshua doesn't like maths.*

**11** ★★ **Das machen Tiere doch nicht! Verneine die folgenden Sätze.**

a) Cats ____________________ bark.

b) Dogs ____________________ talk.

c) Frogs ____________________ ride a bike.

d) Birds ____________________ say Good night.

e) A mouse ____________________ sing.

f) And budgies ____________________ swim.

g) A hamster ____________________ fly.

h) And zebras ____________________ even try.

So when you see a zebra in the sky don't stay, but run away!

**12** ★★ **Setze die Verben in ihrer verneinten Form ins *simple present*.**

a) They ____________________ (not have got) a map of the town.

b) He ____________________ (not know) his way around.

c) We ____________________ (not find) the bus stop.

d) You ____________________ (not have got) the money for the train ticket.

e) The tourist information centre ____________________ (not be) near.

f) She ____________________ (not look at) the sights.

g) They ____________________ (not meet) their tourist guide.

h) The bus ____________________ (not wait) for the tourist group.

**13** ★★ **Es gibt einiges, wofür sich Suzys Mitschüler nicht interessieren. Bilde die Verneinung der angegebenen Verben im *simple present*.**

a) Olivia ______________________ (not be) interested in playing basketball.

b) Daniel ______________________ (not play) computer games.

c) Olivia and Daniel ______________________ (not collect) magazines.

d) Ruby ______________________ (not have got) a guitar.

e) George ______________________ (not go) swimming.

f) Ruby and George ______________________ (not have got) a skateboard.

g) Lucas ______________________ (not draw) pictures.

h) Sophie ______________________ (not like) running.

**14** ★★ **Ergänze den Text mit der richtigen Verbform. Manchmal brauchst du die verneinte Form.**

drive | fly | go | have | invite | live | not / ride | not / walk

Paul Kingsley is a famous pop star. He ________________ in a very big house near London. He ________________ a big swimming pool in his garden and he often ________________ his friends round for a party. He ________________ and he ________________ a bike, either. When he ________________ out, he ________________ an expensive red sports car. Sometimes he even ________________ in his private jet!

## Die Verben *to be* und *to have got*

**15** ★☆ **Was hältst du von Partys? Magst du sie oder magst du sie nicht? Setze die Formen von *to be* ein.**

| | | |
|---|---|---|
| I like parties<br>I don't like parties | because | my friends __________ there.<br>parties __________ a lot of work.<br>it __________ often too noisy there.<br>the music __________ often good.<br>parties __________ a lot of fun.<br>parties __________ very expensive. |

**Tipp**

Das *simple present* ist die einfache Gegenwartsform im Englischen. Die Formen für die beiden wichtigen Verben *to be* und *to have got* lauten so:

| | **to be** | | **to have got** | |
|---|---|---|---|---|
| | Langform | Kurzform | Langform | Kurzform |
| Singular | I am | I'm | I have got | I've got |
| | you are | you're | you have got | you've got |
| | he is | he's | he has got | he's got |
| | she is | she's | she has got | she's got |
| | it is | it's | it has got | it's got |
| Plural | we are | we're | we have got | we've got |
| | you are | you're | you have got | you've got |
| | they are | they're | they have got | they've got |

- Die Langform verwendest du, wenn du etwas schreibst.
- Die Kurzform verwendest du, wenn du sprichst, Gespräche aufschreibst oder an Freunde schreibst.

**16** ★☆ **Ein neuer Schüler stellt sich in der Klasse vor. Schreibe die Kurzformen in Langformen um.**

a) Hi, I'm Danny. ______________________________

b) I'm from Sheffield. ______________________________

c) My parents? They're from Sheffield, too. ______________________________

d) We're new here. ______________________________

e) And who's that in that photo? ______________________________

f) That's my sister. ______________________________

**17** ★★ **Setze die richtigen Formen von *to be* ein. Einige Formen werden verneint.**

Sorry, I ______________ not Ken, I ______________ Tom.

You're from Bristol, right? We ______________ from Bristol, we ______________

from York.

______________ you new here? Yes, we ______________.

______________ the girl over there your sister? No, she ______________.

She ______________ my sister.

______________ Tanya in your class? No, she ______________ in my class.

She ________ in my sister's class.

What about the boys over there? ______________ they in your class? No, they

______________ in my class either.

And the man over there? He ________ our teacher. He ________ our caretaker.

**18** ★★ **Setze die richtigen Langformen von *have got* ein.**

a) Mr and Mrs Benson ____________________ a son.

b) They ____________________ a daughter, too.

c) Mr Benson ____________________ an interesting job.

d) The Bensons ____________________ a house.

e) They ____________________ a car, too.

f) Mrs Benson ____________________ got a sister.

g) She ____________________ a nice house in the country.

h) She ____________________ two children, too.

**19** ★★ **Was ist richtig? Ergänze mit *have got*, *haven't got*, *has got* oder *hasn't got*.**

a) The Owens ____________________ a flat, they ____________________ a house.

b) Their house ____________________ five rooms.

c) David ____________________ a room and Sheila ____________________ a room, too.

d) Danny ____________________ a big room. His room is very small.

e) Mr and Mrs Owen ____________________ a car.

f) Sheila ____________________ a bike.

g) David ____________________ a bike, too.

h) Danny ____________________ a bike because he is too young.

i) But he ____________________ two big toy cars in his room.

**Tipp**

Kurzformen sind Schnellsprechformen, die man vor allem beim Reden und zur Wiedergabe wörtlicher Rede gebraucht. Bei diesen Formen wird *not* zu *-n't*; *has* und *have* werden zu *-'s* und *-'ve* verkürzt. Die Apostrophe zeigen an, dass etwas ausgefallen ist.

Merke:
Bei *haven't* fällt kein *e* aus!

**20** ★★ **Schreibe auf, was sie haben und was nicht.**

| Sam | Ken | The Bensons | Emma |
|---|---|---|---|
| ~~brother~~ | ~~sister~~ | ~~flat~~ | bike |
| aunt | brother | house | ~~car~~ |

Sam ____________ a brother, but ____________ an aunt.

Ken ____________, but ____________.

The Bensons ____________. They ____________.

Emma ____________. She ____________.

**21** ★★ **Setze die passenden Formen von *to be* und *to have* im *simple present* ein.**

a) I ________ Tim. I ________ got a sister.

b) Suzy ________ funny. She ________ got a lot of humour *(Humor)*.

c) Sometimes we ________ got problems and we ________ angry at each other.

d) School ________ okay. All of my friends ________ there, too.

## Modale Hilfsverben

**22** ★☆ **Kreuze an, was den Satz sinnvoll ergänzt.**

a) You ________ text* and ride your bike. It's too dangerous.

☐ mustn't ☐ needn't

b) She ________ go to bed now. She can go later.

☐ mustn't ☐ needn't

c) I ________ wash my hands. They aren't dirty.

☐ mustn't ☐ needn't

d) Philip ________ drink milk. He's allergic to it.

☐ mustn't ☐ needn't

e) We ________ forget our pencils. We need them for the test.

☐ mustn't ☐ needn't

* to text: eine SMS schreiben

**Tipp**

Können, müssen, dürfen, sollen sind modale Hilfsverben. Sie drücken aus, ob ich zum Beispiel meine Hausaufgaben machen muss, machen kann, machen darf oder machen soll.

Diese Hilfsverben gibt es auch im Englischen (engl.: *modal auxiliaries*). Dies sind die Hilfsverben, die du bisher gelernt hast:

| | | | |
|---|---|---|---|
| can | können, dürfen | can't / cannot | nicht können |
| must | müssen | mustn't | nicht dürfen |
| may | dürfen | needn't | nicht müssen, nicht brauchen |
| shall | sollen | | |

**23** ★☆ **Setze das richtige Hilfsverb ein. Was du in der Schule tun musst ...**

a) I ______________________ do my homework. (muss)

b) I ______________________talk all the time. (darf nicht)

c) I ______________________ make my teachers angry. (muss nicht)

d) I ______________________ sing in the English lesson. (brauche nicht)

e) I ______________________ go home when I want. (kann nicht)

**Tipp**

Bei Fragen mit Hilfsverben steht das Hilfsverb vor dem Subjekt. Nach dem Subjekt steht immer der Infinitiv.
Bei Kurzfragen wird das Hilfsverb in der Antwort wiederholt. Die verneinte Form von *must* ist *needn't*.

**24** ★★ **Du bist heute krank und stellst deinem Arzt eine Menge Fragen. Gib seine Kurzantworten.**

a) Must I go to school? *No,* ______________________________________.

b) Must I stay in bed all day? *Yes,* ______________________________________.

c) Must I do my homework? *No,* ______________________________________.

d) May I get up tomorrow? *No,* ______________________________________.

e) Must I take my temperature? *Yes,* ______________________________________.

f) Can I call my friends? *Yes,* ______________________________________.

g) May my friends come and see me? *Yes,* ______________________, but not today.

**25** ★★ **Tim bereitet sich gerade auf einen mehrtägigen Schulausflug nach Brighton vor. In dem Dialog mit seinen Eltern ist jeweils nur eines der angegebenen modalen Hilfsverben passend. Streiche das unpassende Modalverb durch.**

a) *Tim:* "*Shall / Must* I take my boots or my trainers with me? What do you think, Mum?"

b) *Mum:* "Well, you *can / mustn't* pack both into your suitcase *(Koffer)*, Tim. It is big enough for both."

c) *Dad:* "But remember that you *must / needn't* carry your suitcase all the way to the bus station, so do not put too much into it!"

d) *Tim:* "All right, Dad. *Shall / May* I borrow your new windbreaker *(Windjacke)* then? It is very light, isn't it?"

e) *Dad:* "Okay, Tim, but you *must / could* remember that it is not only a very light but also a very expensive jacket."

f) *Tim:* "I know that, Dad. You *mustn't / needn't* worry."

g) *Mum:* "And Tim, you *mustn't / must* forget your mobile."

h) *Tim:* "How *shall / could* I forget my mobile? It's already in my bag."

i) *Mum:* "Good, *could / may* you then call us every day, please?"

j) *Tim:* "Oh Mum, I really *can / cannot* do that. But I *can / needn't* send you a short text message instead *(stattdessen)*."

k) *Mum:* "Well, is there anything else we *must / can* do for you?"

l) *Tim:* "Yes Mum, you and Dad *cannot / mustn't* give me any more tips for the trip …"

**26** ★★ **Sicher kennst du die folgenden Verhaltensregeln aus deiner eigenen Schule. Vervollständige die Sätze jeweils mit der englischen Entsprechung des in Klammern angegebenen Hilfsverbs.**

a) Pupils ______________________ *(nicht müssen)* sit on the floor.

b) But they ______________________ *(nicht dürfen)* throw rubbish on the floor.

c) Teachers ______________________ *(dürfen)* control the pupils' homework.

d) But they ______________________ *(nicht müssen)* do the homework for their pupils.

e) Pupils ______________________ *(können)* have a break between lessons.

f) But they ______________________ *(nicht dürfen)* sleep during lessons.

g) Pupils ______________________ *(müssen)* respect each other *(gegenseitig)*.

h) But they ______________________ *(nicht müssen)* love each other.

i) Parents ______________________ *(können)* help their children with their homework.

j) But they ______________________ *(nicht können)* write the school tests for their children.

**27** ★★ **David ist als Austauschschüler bei Familie Carter und will besonders höflich sein. Setze *may*, *may not*, *can* oder *can't* ein.**

a) *David:* "Mrs Carter, _______________ I have another bowl of soup, please?"

b) *Mrs Carter:* "Yes, of course you _______________."

c) *David:* "There is a party at school today. _______________ I go, please?"

d) *Mrs Carter:* "No, you _______________ go alone.

e) But you _______________ take your friend Justin with you."

## Der Imperativ

**28** ★☆ **Gebrauche den Imperativ! Verwende die folgenden Verben:**

be · be · tidy · be · wash · go · buy

a) Your room looks a mess! ________________ it up, please!

b) Can you do me a favour? ________________ to the butcher's and ________________ some sausages there.

c) But ________________ back soon. Don't ________________ late.

d) Let's have supper now. But ________________ your hands before we eat.

e) Are you going out tonight? ________________ back until 8 o'clock.

**Tipp**

Um Gebote und Verbote auszudrücken, kannst du die Befehlsform, d.h. den Imperativ, gebrauchen. Dabei musst du zwischen den bejahten und den verneinten Formen des Imperativs unterscheiden:

| Bejahte Formen: | Verneinte Formen: |
| --- | --- |
| Go home, David! | Don't go home, David! |
| Go home, David and Mike! | Don't go home, David and Mike! |
| Go home, Mr Mason! | Don't go home, Mr Mason! |

Die bejahten Formen werden mit dem Infinitiv ohne *to*, die verneinten Formen mit *don't* + Infinitiv ohne *to* gebildet. Die Formen für den Singular und den Plural sowie für die Höflichkeitsform sind jeweils gleich.

**29** ★☆

**Amys Klasse besucht den Zoo. Der Lehrer gibt ihnen einige Regeln mit. Formuliere die Gebote und Verbote im Imperativ.**

a) not / run / around alone

______________________________

b) wait / for the group

______________________________

c) not / feed / the animals

______________________________

d) not / throw / anything

______________________________

**Tipp**

Auch der verneinte Imperativ von *to be* wird mit *don't* gebildet:

*Be careful!* *Don't be silly!*

**30** ★★

**Bilde Imperative und verwende verneinte Formen, wo sie sinnvoll sind.**

a) forget your homework ______________________________

b) talk to your neighbour ______________________________

c) listen to me ______________________________

d) be late ______________________________

e) do your homework now, do it later ______________________________

f) be so loud ______________________________

## Fragen mit Kurzantworten

**31** ★☆ **Musst du *do* oder *does* ergänzen? Vervollständige die Fragen.**

a) ________________ the holidays start on July 5th or 6th?

b) ________________ Phoebe live in London or in Cambridge?

c) How ________________ you spell your name?

d) ________________ Jeff have fried eggs for breakfast?

e) Why ________________ Fiona always buy sweets after school?

f) How ________________ you make pizza bread?

**Tipp**

Entscheidungsfragen werden auch Ja/Nein-Fragen genannt, weil du entweder mit Ja oder mit Nein darauf antwortest. Wenn du ein Vollverb verwendest, z. B. *play* oder *like*, dann bildest du diese Fragen mit *do/does*.

*Do you play tennis?*
*Does Lauren like chocolate ice cream?*

**32** ★☆ **Vervollständige die Fragen, und beantworte sie.**

a) ________ your brother ________ a computer? – Yes, he ________.

b) ________ your parents ________ a new car? – No, ________________.

They ________ still ________ their old car.

c) ________ your teacher ________ a new baby? – No, he ________________.

## 33 ★☆ Markiere, welche Antwort richtig formuliert ist.

a) Does Billy eat a lot of sweets?

☐ Yes, he eats. ☐ Yes, he does.

b) Do you have a sister?

☐ No, you don't. ☐ No, I don't.

c) Does Mrs Jones teach English?

☐ No, she doesn't. ☐ No, she don't.

d) Do your parents work in the city?

☐ Yes, she does. ☐ No, they don't.

e) Does Louise know the answer to this question?

☐ Yes, she does. ☐ Yes, she knows.

**Tipp**

Wenn du mit *to have got* Fragen stellst und eine Kurzantwort gibst, sieht das folgendermaßen aus:

*Has Sheila got a sister? No, she hasn't.*
*Have the Owens got a car? Yes, they have.*

## 34 ★☆ Gib Kurzantworten.

a) Isn't that Mr Mason? *Yes,* ______________________.

b) Isn't he your English teacher? *Yes,* ______________________.

c) Aren't you happy to see him? *No,* ______________________.

d) Is that your school cafeteria? *Yes,* ______________________.

e) What about the food there? Is it good? *No,* ______________________.

f) Are there any good restaurants here? *No,* ______________________.

g) Is that a good restaurant? *No,* ______________________.

h) Are you hungry? *Yes,* ______________________.

**35** ★☆ **Schreibe Kurzantworten zu den Fragen.**

**Beispiel:** Does Lucy like chocolate? *Yes, she does.*

a) Do Julie and Chris live in Frankfurt? *No,* ______________________

b) Does Lara play the guitar? *No,* ______________________

c) Do you go to St Mary's School? *Yes,* ______________________

d) Does your dog like walks? *Yes,* ______________________

e) Do we have English homework today? *No,* ______________________

**Tipp**

Als Erwiderung auf Entscheidungsfragen sagt man im Englischen nicht einfach „*Yes.*" oder „*No.*", denn das klingt ziemlich unhöflich. Vielmehr benutzt man Kurzantworten, und zwar nach *yes* mit *do/does* und nach *no* mit *don't/doesn't*.

*Do you want to go to the music shop? – Yes, I do.*

*Does Harry tidy his room every week? – No, he doesn't.*

**36** ★☆ **Ergänze die Kurzantworten. Das Pluszeichen (+) steht für eine bejahende Antwort, das Minuszeichen (–) für eine verneinende.**

a) Do you go jogging in the morning? (+) *Yes,* ______________________.

b) Does Mrs White work in a shop? (–) *No,* ______________________.

c) Hi, you two. Do you want to play streetball with us? (+)

______________________.

d) Does Tyler like rap music? (+) ______________________.

**37** ★☆ **Setze die richtigen Formen von *to be* ein und gib Sarahs Antworten.**

a) ________ it your birthday party? No, ________________________________.

b) ________ David's sister at your party? Yes, ________________________________.

c) ________ your parents out? Yes, ________________________________.

d) ________ there any girls from your class here? Yes, ________________________________.

e) ________ you and Sheila in David's class? No, ________________________________.

**38** ★★ **Die Freundinnen stellen Sheila ein paar Fragen. Bilde ihre Fragen und gib dann die entsprechenden Kurzantworten.**

**Beispiel:** you / from Fulford?

*Are you from Fulford?*

*No, I'm not.*

a) you / from York?

________________________________________________________________?

*Yes,* ________________________________________________________________.

b) your parents / from York, too?

________________________________________________________________?

*Yes,* ________________________________________________________________.

c) you / often in Fulford?

________________________________________________________________?

*Yes,* ________________________________________________________________.

**39** ★★ **Deine Familie! Stelle Fragen, und gib dann die Kurzantworten.**

| | | | |
|---|---|---|---|
| **Has**<br>Have | you<br>your parents<br>your mother<br>**your father**<br>your English teacher<br>your boyfriend<br>your friends | **got** | a hamster?<br>a girlfriend?<br>**an elephant?**<br>a taxi?<br>a dog?<br>a teddy?<br>a football? |

**Beispiel:** *Has your father got an elephant? – No, he hasn't.*

______________________________

______________________________

______________________________

______________________________

______________________________

______________________________

______________________________

**40** ★★ **Übersetze die Fragen.**

a) Wohnst du in London Road?

______________________________

b) Spielt John Basketball?

______________________________

c) Essen Alex und Andy Käse?

______________________________

**41** ★★ **Sortiere die Wörter so, dass sie Fragen ergeben. Schreibe die Fragen dann richtig auf.**

a) want – you – an ice cream – do – ?

______________________________

b) Ellie – her teachers – does – like – ?

______________________________

c) does – buy – James – his jeans – where – ?

______________________________

d) Mrs Seth – when – do the shopping – does – ?

______________________________

e) you – do – in the morning – watch TV – ?

______________________________

f) does – start – your first lesson – when – ?

______________________________

g) at the school cafeteria – do – have lunch – you – ?

______________________________

h) Amar – want – a pet – does – ?

______________________________

i) you – a lot of film stars – do – know – ?

______________________________

## Fragen mit Fragewörtern

**42** ★☆ **Welches Fragewort passt jeweils in die Lücke? Ergänze *where*, *who*, *what* oder *how*.**

a) ______________ is the date today? – It's 27th May.

b) ______________ are you? – I'm fine, thanks.

c) ______________ is your homework? – It's at home. Sorry!

d) ______________ is in the kitchen? – That's my dad.

e) ______________ is Felix? – He's in the playground.

f) ______________ is Felix? – He's a boy in my class.

**Tipp**

Bestimmungsfragen werden mit Fragewörtern wie *when*, *what*, *where*, *why* und *how* gebildet. Danach folgt wieder *do* oder *does*.

*When do you get up in the morning?*
*What does Ethan do in the evening?*
*Where do you buy CDs?*

**43** ★☆ **Mit welchen Fragewörtern fragst du nach dem Subjekt, Objekt usw.? Trage sie in die Tabelle ein.**

| | | | | |
|---|---|---|---|---|
| Debbie | sees | Tom | in the classroom | at 9. |
| The shop | shows | its top cars | in its showrooms | this week. |
| **Subjekt** | **Verb** | **Objekt** | **Ort** | **Zeit** |
| a) ________ | | a) ________ | | |
| b) ________ | ________ | b) ________ | ________ | ________ |

**44** ★★ **Verbinde die Fragen mit den passenden Antworten. Pass genau auf, dass du die beiden Fragewörter *where* (Wo?) und *who* (Wer?) nicht verwechselst.**

| | |
|---|---|
| a) Where is the dog? | They're on the football team. |
| b) Who is Mr Braun? | I don't know her name. |
| c) Where's your classroom? | It's in the garden, under the tree. |
| d) Who are those boys? | He's my cousin. |
| e) Where are the sandwiches? | They're in your bag. |
| f) Who is Luke? | He's my German teacher. |
| g) Where are my books? | It's upstairs on the left. |
| h) Who is that girl? | They're in the kitchen. |

**45** ★★ **Stelle Fragen.**

a) Where / you / live?

________________________________________?

b) Where / your parents / work?

________________________________________?

c) When / they / get up?

________________________________________?

d) When / you get up?

________________________________________?

e) When / your lessons / begin?

________________________________________?

# 2 Present progressive

## Das Partizip Präsens

**Tipp**

Das *present participle* wird mit dem Infinitiv und der Endung *-ing* gebildet:
to talk → talking    to speak → speaking

Endet der Infinitiv auf einen Konsonanten, so wird dieser verdoppelt:
to swim → swimming    to cut → cutting

Endet er auf ein stummes *-e*, entfällt dieses; endet er auf *-ie*, wird diese Silbe zu *-y*:
to slice → slicing    to lie → lying

**1** ★☆ **Bilde das Partizip Präsens der folgenden Verben.**

clean ______________________ wash ______________________

sing ______________________ laugh ______________________

talk ______________________ fight ______________________

drink ______________________ eat ______________________

listen ______________________ shout ______________________

knock ______________________ do ______________________

watch ______________________ fix ______________________

go ______________________ buy ______________________

play ______________________ say ______________________

cry ______________________ try ______________________

carry ______________________ look ______________________

**2** ★☆ **Achtung bei der Bildung des Partizip Präsens bei den folgenden Verben!**

write ______________________

lose ______________________

ride ______________________

change ______________________

drive ______________________

plan ______________________

sit ______________________

run ______________________

stop ______________________

cut ______________________

forget ______________________

die ______________________

slice ______________________

choose ______________________

come ______________________

take ______________________

have ______________________

trip ______________________

put ______________________

clap ______________________

drop ______________________

swim ______________________

get ______________________

lie ______________________

tie ______________________

travel ______________________

## Das *present progressive*

**3** ★☆

**a) Bilde Sätze im *present progressive* mit den angegebenen Verben.**

The sun ______________________________ (shine).

It's not ______________________________ (rain).

The birds ______________________________ (sing).

And we ______________________________ (sit) indoors!

We ______________________________ (do) a test.

Look! Mike ______________________________ (dream).

He ______________________________ (listen) to the birds.

Our teacher ______________________________ (try) to talk to Mike.

**b) Erkläre, warum du hier das *present progressive* gebrauchen musst.**

______________________________________________

______________________________________________

**Tipp**

Im Gegensatz zum *simple present* gebraucht man das *present progressive* für Handlungen, die zu einem bestimmten Zeitpunkt der Gegenwart noch nicht vorbei sind, sondern noch stattfinden.

*Look! Mike is looking at his photos.*
*He is watching them on his computer now.*

Die entsprechenden Signalwörter lauten:

| | | | |
|---|---|---|---|
| *at this moment* | in diesem Moment | *now* | jetzt |
| *this morning* | heute Morgen | *today* | heute |
| *this afternoon* | heute Nachmittag | *look!* | schau! |
| *this evening* | heute Abend | *listen!* | hör zu! |

**4** ★☆ **Familie Smith verbringt einen Tag am Strand. Setze die Verben in Klammern ins *present progressive*.**

a) The Smiths ______________________ *(spend)* a weekend at the seaside in Brighton.

b) They ______________________ (have) a lot of fun on the beach.

c) Tim ______________________ (chase) Suzy in the water.

d) Mrs Smith ______________________ (buy) some ice-cream.

e) Mr Smith ______________________ (read) a book.

f) A lot of other people ______________________ (enjoy: *genießen*) their time on the beach, too.

g) A little child ______________________ (build) a sand castle.

h) An old man ______________________ (try) to catch a fish.

i) A girl ______________________ (drink) a bottle of cold coke.

j) Another girl ______________________ (draw) a picture of the sea.

k) A woman ______________________ (sleep) on her sunbed (Liegestuhl).

l) A boy ______________________ (look) at a sailing boat.

m) His brother ______________________ (call) his girl-friend.

n) Some teenagers ______________________ (play) volleyball.

o) A dog ______________________ (swim) in the water.

**5** ★☆

**Welche Signalwörter kannst du nicht mit dem *present progressive* gebrauchen?**

next year | listen! | this morning | then | at this moment | just

this afternoon | today | look! | now | this evening

the next day | every morning | after that | the next evening | seldom

**6** ★★

**Verbessere die Fehler in diesen Sätzen.**

a) Bill is geting up now.

______________________________

b) I writing a birthday card for Jamie.

______________________________

c) All the children are danceing.

______________________________

d) Rosie feeling tired.

______________________________

e) We are haveing a nice time.

______________________________

f) They are puting their books on the desk.

______________________________

g) I am listenning to a CD.

______________________________

**7** ★★ **Die Schüler sind im Klassenzimmer, aber ihr Lehrer ist noch nicht da. Schreibe auf, was sie nicht tun.**

a) The pupils (not sit) in their chairs.

________________________________________

b) They (not do) their exercises.

________________________________________

c) They (not take) notes.

________________________________________

d) They (not look) at their exercise books.

________________________________________

e) They (not work).

________________________________________

f) Tom (not sleep).

________________________________________

g) Mike (not flirt) with Alice.

________________________________________

**Tipp**

Wenn du die Verlaufsform verneinst, stellst du einfach *not* hinter die Form von *to be*. Danach folgt die *-ing*-Form.

Langform: *Mick is not sleeping.*
Kurzform: *Maggie isn't playing computer games.*

**8** ★★ **Setze die Verben in ihrer verneinten Form ins *present progressive*.**

a) I ______________________ (not go) for a run.

b) You ______________________ (not swim) in the sea.

c) We ______________________ (not dance) at the club.

d) They ______________________ (not jump) into the water.

e) He ______________________ (not climb) the rock.

f) You ______________________ (not kick) the ball.

g) She ______________________ (not fight) to win.

**9** ★★ **Bilde aus den folgenden Sätzen verneinte Aussagesätze.**

**Beispiel:** I'm starting my homework. *I'm not starting my homework.*

a) Maggie's running in the park.

______________________________________________

b) We're helping our mum.

______________________________________________

c) The children are answering the questions.

______________________________________________

d) You're talking about the football match.

______________________________________________

**10** ★★ **Was machen Amelie, Jack und Marc gerade? Schreibe bejahte oder verneinte Aussagesätze.**

| | Amelie | Jack and Marc |
|---|---|---|
| watch TV | ✗ | ✓ |
| read book | ✓ | ✗ |
| try on shoes | ✗ | ✓ |
| buy a magazine | ✓ | ✗ |

a) *Amelie isn't watching TV.* ______________________

b) *Jack and Marc* ______________________

c) ______________________

d) ______________________

e) ______________________

f) ______________________

g) ______________________

h) ______________________

**Tipp**

Besonderheiten bei der Schreibung der *ing*-Form:

- Ein stummes e am Ende des Verbs fällt weg.
  take + *ing* → taking
  write + *ing* → writing
- Endet das Verb auf Konsonant nach einem betonten Kurzvokal, verdoppelt sich der Konsonant.
  run + *ing* → running
  get + *ing* → getting

## Fragen mit Kurzantworten

**11** ★☆ **Der Lehrer stellt einige Fragen. Gib die entsprechenden Kurzantworten.**

**Beispiel:** Are you listening, Mike? **(Yes)** Yes, I am.

a) What are you doing, David? Are you writing a letter to Susan? **(No)**

_______________

b) Are you doing your homework, Robert? **(No)**

_______________

c) Where are Bill and Kevin? Are they looking for the classroom? **(Yes)**

_______________

d) Where is your book, Al? Is it still lying on the floor? **(No)**

_______________

e) Are you dreaming of your holidays, John and Ann? **(No)**

_______________

**Tipp**

Bei Fragen steht im *present progressive* zunächst eine Form von *to be*, dann das Subjekt and schließlich das *present participle*.

Bei Kurzantworten wird das *present participle* ausgelassen. Ansonsten gilt auch hier die Regel:

*Yes,* + Pronomen + bejahte Langform
*No,* + Pronomen + verneinte Kurzform

| | | | |
|---|---|---|---|
| Are | you | listening? | Yes, I am. |
| Are | you | talking? | No, I'm not. |
| Is | David | talking? | Yes, he is. |
| Is | Sheila | sleeping? | No, she isn't. |

**12** ★☆ **Fragen über Fragen! Gib die entsprechenden Kurzantworten.**

a) Are you doing this test now? *Yes,* ______________________.

b) Are your parents helping you? *No,* ______________________.

c) Is your sister / brother helping you? *No,* ______________________.

d) Are your teachers helping you? *No,* ______________________.

e) Are you listening to music? *No,* ______________________.

**13** ★☆ **Was machen die Goodmans gerade? Lies und antworte mit Kurzantworten wie zum Beispiel: *Yes, he is. / No, they aren't.***

It's 6 p.m. in the Goodmans' house. Tony is watching TV. Abby is washing her hair. Peter is finishing his homework. Dad is cleaning the kitchen. Mum is checking her e-mails. Grandpa is sleeping in his favourite chair. The dogs are playing with a ball.

a) Is Tony watching TV? ______________________

b) Is Dad working in the garage? ______________________

c) Are Abby and Peter listening to music? ______________________

d) Is Mum checking her e-mails? ______________________

e) Is Grandpa sleeping in his bed? ______________________

f) Are the dogs eating their dinner? ______________________

g) Is Peter doing his homework? ______________________

h) Is Abby washing her hair? ______________________

## 14 ★☆ Vervollständige die Fragen und beantworte sie.

a) ______________ you waiting for me? – Yes, ____________________.

b) ______________ he looking for his jacket? – No, ____________________.

c) ______________ I using your pen? – No, ____________________.

d) ______________ they winning the match? – Yes, ____________________.

e) ______________ your dog barking out there? – Yes, ____________________.

f) ______________ we finishing the lesson now? – No, ____________________.

g) ______________ Catherine eating spaghetti? – No, ____________________.

## 15 ★★ Der Lehrer betritt den Klassenraum. Was tun die Schülerinnen und Schüler gerade? Bilde Fragen.

a) Tom / sit / in* his chair? ______________________________________________?

b) He / do / an exercise? ______________________________________________?

c) Kevin and Ken / make / girls angry? ______________________________________________

______________________________________________?

d) Alice / flirt / with Mike? ______________________________________________?

e) Robert / lie / on the floor? ______________________________________________?

f) Ben and John / play / cards? ______________________________________________?

g) Debbie / read / a magazine? ______________________________________________?

h) Fiona / run / around the classroom? ______________________________________________

______________________________________________?

* Man kann sowohl *to sit in a chair* als auch *to sit on a chair* sagen. Beides ist richtig.

**16** ★★ **Was passiert auf dem Schulfest? Wandle die Aussagesätze in Fragen um. Setze dabei das Verb in Klammern ins *present progressive*.**

**Beispiel:** Kylie (listen) to some of the pupils. *Is Kylie listening to some of the pupils?*

a) They (play) the drums.

______________________________

b) She (sit) next to her friend Amy.

______________________________

c) Jack (show) his parents the classrooms.

______________________________

d) The English teacher (dance) with the Maths teacher.

______________________________

**17** ★★ **Übersetze die Fragen. Verwende die Verlaufsform, also das *present progressive*.**

a) Sitzt die Katze auf dem Stuhl?

______________________________

b) Springen die Kinder auf dem Bett?

______________________________

c) Essen wir heute Fisch?

______________________________

## Fragen mit Fragewörtern

**18** ★☆

**Stelle Fragen im *present progressive* mit Fragewörtern.**

a) Where you / go? ______________________________?

b) What you / do? ______________________________?

c) Why / you / not listen? ______________________________?

d) Who / talk? ______________________________?

e) What / you / read? ______________________________?

f) Why / you / leave the room? ______________________________?

g) Why you / not take notes? ______________________________?

h) Why / you / not / do this exercise? ______________________________

______________________________________________?

**Tipp**

Wie bei allen Verbformen sind auch bei der Verlaufsform des Präsens Fragen mit Fragewörtern möglich. Diese Fragewörter werden einfach vor die entsprechende Form von *to be* gesetzt. Danach folgt das Subjekt, danach das *present participle*.

Mit *who* fragt man nach Personen, mit *what* nach Sachen, mit *where* nach dem Ort oder der Richtung, mit *when* nach der Zeit und mit *why* nach dem Grund. Mit *how* fragt man nach der Art und Weise, wie etwas geschieht. Verwechsle im Übrigen nicht *who* (= wer) mit *where* (= wo / wohin).

*What is she doing?*
*Where are they going?*

**19** ★★ **Schreibe die folgenden Fragen an einen bekannten Schauspieler, bei denen es um die Oscar-Party geht, in der richtigen Reihenfolge auf.**

a) wearing – what – your wife – was – at the party

___

b) who – sitting – at your table – was – with you

___

c) for dinner – were – you – having – what

___

d) laughing – you – why – so much – were

___

**20** ★★ **In London gibt es eine Menge Leute zu beobachten. Frage nach dem unterstrichenen Satzteil.**

a) This woman is reading a book <u>on the tube</u>.

___

b) That woman is drinking <u>a cup of tea</u>.

___

c) This man is buying <u>a chicken sandwich</u>.

___

d) That man is laughing <u>because of a joke</u>.

___

**21** ★★ **Danny ist von der Schule nach Hause gekommen. Frage nach den fett hervorgehobenen Wörtern.**

**Beispiel:** It's two o'clock. Danny is in his room. **He** is lying **on the floor**.

*Who is lying on the floor? Where is he lying?*

a) He is doing **his homework**.

______________________________________________

b) He's got David's German exercise book and he is doing **an exercise**.

______________________________________________

c) **He** is drawing a picture.

______________________________________________

d) He is singing a song **because he is happy**.

______________________________________________

e) There's some chocolate in his hands. He is eating **it**.

______________________________________________

f) Suddenly there is a noise. **Somebody** is coming upstairs.

______________________________________________

g) It's David. He **is looking** for his exercise book.

______________________________________________

h) He is angry. He **is shouting** at Danny.

______________________________________________

## 22 ★★ Verbinde die Fragen mit den passenden Antworten.

| | |
|---|---|
| a) What are you playing? | Andy. |
| b) Where are you going? | Very happy! |
| c) What are you eating? | Basketball. |
| d) Who are you talking to? | My German book. |
| e) What are you looking for? | A photo of Molly's cat. |
| f) How are you feeling? | To town. |
| g) What are you doing? | A sandwich. |
| h) What are you looking at? | I'm reading a text from Tim. |

## 23 ★★ Setze *who* oder *where* ein und beantworte dann die Frage.

**Beispiel:** *Where* is Sheila? (at school) *She is at school.*

a) ___________ is writing a maths test? (Sheila)

___________________________________________

b) ___________ is her maths book? (under her desk)

___________________________________________

c) ___________ is she looking at? (her teacher)

___________________________________________

d) ___________ is he looking at? (her)

___________________________________________

## Verben mit Präpositionen

**24** ★☆ **Füge die entsprechende Präposition zu den Verben hinzu.**

a) What are you looking ______________________? (suchen)

b) Who are you waiting ______________________? (warten)

c) Who are you looking ______________________? (ansehen)

d) What are you listening ______________________? (zuhören)

e) What are you talking ______________________? (reden über)

f) Who are you looking ______________________? (sich kümmern um)

g) Who are you thinking ______________________? (denken an)

h) Why are you running ______________________? (wegrennen)

i) What are you writing ______________________? (aufschreiben)

j) What word are you looking ______________________? (nachschlagen)

k) What trousers are you trying ______________________? (anprobieren)

**25** ★★ **Was ist das Gegenteil? Setze die richtige Präposition ein.**

| | |
|---|---|
| a) to get on a bus | to get ______________________ a bus |
| b) to turn a radio on | to turn it ______________________ |
| c) to put on a shirt | to take it ______________________ |
| d) to take off your clothes | to put them ______________________ |
| e) to fall asleep | to wake ______________________ |

## Besondere Verben

**Tipp**

Nicht alle Verben kommen im present progressive vor. Verben, die Zustände oder Sinneswahrnehmungen beschreiben, werden normalerweise nicht im *present progressive* gebraucht. Solche Verben sind:

| | | | | |
|---|---|---|---|---|
| to be | to hate | to hear | to need | to like |
| to think | to love | to see | to know | to want |

Bei diesen Verben musst du das *simple present* verwenden.

**26** ★★ **Sheila hat einen Hund bekommen. Muss das *simple present* oder das *present progressive* eingesetzt werden? Ergänze.**

After a long fight with her parents Sheila has a pet! It's not that her parents ______________ (not like) pets, but Mrs Owen ____________________ (think) that she has already got three children and that she ______________ __________ (not need) another baby to look after. So Sheila must look after it, buy its food and take it for a walk every day. You already know what pet it is. It's a dog. Its name is Bingo. Bingo is a small dog, but he's young and full of life. He always ______________ (run) around and like most small dogs he ______________ (bark) a lot. Can you hear him? He ________________ (bark) now! Sometimes this is a problem because not everybody ______________ (like) to hear him in the middle of the night. This is a problem for Bingo, too because he can't understand why his people _________________________ (throw) shoes at him or _________________________ (shout) at him when he only __________________ (want) to warn them against burglars *(Einbrecher)*.

# 3 Simple present oder present progressive?

**1** ★☆ **Einfache Gegenwart oder Verlaufsform? Schreibe das Verb in der richtigen Form in die Lücke.**

a) We ________________ a lot of fun at this party. (have)

b) I sometimes ________________ by plane. (travel)

c) "Where are the boys?" "They ________________ in the sea." (swim)

d) ________ you ________________ this video? (watch)

e) ________ you always ________________ lunch at school? (eat)

f) Martin ________________ early on Monday mornings. (get up)

g) It's late. I ________________ to bed now. (go)

**Tipp**

Zwischen dem *simple present* und dem *present progressive* gibt es wichtige Unterschiede.

*simple present*
- beschreibt Zustände
- beschreibt Gewohnheiten
- beschreibt regelmäßige Handlungen
- beschreibt aufeinander folgende Handlungen, z.B. in einer Geschichte

Signalwörter: *every day/morning/week …, always, often, usually, normally, sometimes, never*

*present progressive*
- beschreibt, was im Moment gerade passiert

Signalwörter: *at the moment, at present, (right) now, just, look!*

*He usually sleeps at 6 o'clock, but today he is jogging.*

**2** ★☆ **Welche Zeit muss hier verwendet werden? Kreuze die richtige Form des Verbs an.**

a) Jonas ________ football every Wednesday afternoon.

☐ plays ☐ is playing

b) Fiona ________ the guitar in her bedroom.

☐ plays ☐ is playing

c) I ________ eggs because I ________ them.

☐ don't eat / don't like ☐ am not eating / am not liking

d) We ________ eggs today. We ________ chicken.

☐ don't eat / eat ☐ aren't eating / are eating

e) "What are you doing?" "I ________ my dad in the garden."

☐ help ☐ am helping

**3** ★☆ ***Simple present* oder *present progressive*? Beantworte die Fragen.**

a) Doesn't Mr Brown live here? – No, he doesn't. He ____________________ in London now. (live)

b) Can you talk to me, Bob? – Sorry, not now, I ____________________ the football match on TV. (watch)

c) Look! That's Bobby's team. They ____________________ against another school. (play)

____________________ you ____________________ football, too? (play)

d) Tom, where are you? – In my room.

What ____________________ you ____________________ there? (do)

I ____________________ very busy (be). I ____________________ my homework. (do)

**4** ★☆ **Lily, die Katze der Familie Smith, ist allein zu Haus. Entscheide, ob du das *simple present* oder das *present progressive* der angegebenen Verben in die Lücken einsetzen musst.**

a) Lily ______________________ (like) milk a lot.

b) Look, she ______________________ (drink) her milk now.

c) She ______________________ (be) very thirsty.

d) So she ______________________ (want) some more.

e) But she ______________________ (not can) get more milk,

f) because there ______________________ (be) nobody at home.

g) Now Lily ______________________ (try) to open the fridge,

h) but she ______________________ (not can) do that.

i) So she ______________________ (must) think of something else.

j) First she ______________________ (have) a look at the breakfast table.

k) But there ______________________ (not be) any milk left (übrig).

l) Then she ______________________ (climb: klettern) onto the cupboard in the living room.

m) But she ______________________ (not be) lucky.

n) Finally she ______________________ (not know) what else (was noch) to try.

o) Now she ______________________ (wait) until the Smiths come home.

**5** ★☆ ***Simple present* oder *present progressive*? Setze die richtigen Formen ein.**

Today ______________________________ (be) Kim's birthday. All her friends

______________________________ (want) to come to her party. So Kim and

her family ______________________________ (be) very busy. At the moment

Kim and her sister, Annabel, ______________________________ (decorate)

the living room. Kim ______________________________ (like) colourful balloons and

candles. Her father ______________________________ (buy) juice,

food and sweets at the supermarket. Her mum ______________________________

(make) sandwiches in the kitchen. Kim ______________________________ (feel)

happy. She ______________________________ (think) that everything

______________________________ (be) great.

**Tipp**

Beachte:
Das *present progressive* kannst du nur für Handlungen und Vorgänge verwenden: *eat, walk, write, listen*

Eine ganze Reihe von Verben kommt nur im *simple present*, nicht im *present progressive* vor,
- darunter Verben der Wahrnehmung: *hear, see, feel*
- und Verben, mit denen man Gefühle, Meinungen und Wünsche ausdrückt: *like, think* (meinen), *want*

Auch *to be* erscheint in der Regel im *simple present*.

## 6 ★★ Setze die Verben in der richtigen Form ein.

a) It ________________ (be) Saturday morning and Tim ________________ (clean) his room at the moment. He usually ________________ (play) with his friends on Saturdays but today he ________________ (stay) at home because his mother ________________ (be) angry with him.

b) Mr and Mrs Weaver ________________ (like) action films. So they often ________________ (go) to the cinema together. But today they ________________ (watch) an exciting film on TV.

c) On Monday afternoons Sam and Kevin often ________________ (play) tennis. But today Kevin ________________ (study) for a test and Sam ________________ (shop) with his sister, Carol. Sam ________________ (need) new shoes and Carol ________________ (know) a lot of good shops.

d) Peter: "Look! That cat over there ________________ (want) to take a bath in the pond."

Mick: "No, cats ________________ (hate) water. This cat ________________ (try) to catch a fish."

Peter: "Oh, you ________________ (be) right."

**7** ★★ **Bilde Sätze mit dem *simple present* oder dem *present progressive*.**

a) Mrs Owen / work / at the Tourist Information Centre.

______________________________________________

b) She / help / tourists.

______________________________________________

c) Sometimes she / help / them find a hotel.

______________________________________________

d) She / answer / their questions.

______________________________________________

e) She / give / them all kind of information about York.

______________________________________________

f) Today / she / be / there again.

______________________________________________

g) A lot of people / wait / for her.

______________________________________________

h) They / want / to ask her a lot of questions.

______________________________________________

i) A tourist / ask / her for the way to the station.

______________________________________________

**8** ★★ **In manche Sätze haben sich Fehler eingeschlichen. Schreibe die Sätze richtig auf.**

**Beispiel:** We are having an English lesson every Tuesday morning.

*We have an English lesson every Tuesday morning.*

a) I'm just listening to a great song.

______________________________

b) The children take a test this morning.

______________________________

c) Melanie never gets up before 7 o'clock.

______________________________

d) Look, Daniel wears his new jacket.

______________________________

**9** ★★ **Ergänze den Dialog mit den richtigen Verben.**

buy | come | give | go | go | wait

*Lucy:* Oh, hi, Mia. ________ you ______________ for the Number 3 bus, too?

*Mia:* Hi, Lucy, yes, I am. Where ________ you ______________?

*Lucy:* I ______________ to town.

*Mia:* Me too! I often ______________ something on Saturdays because my mum ______________ me money at the weekend.

*Lucy:* That's nice. Oh, look! The bus ______________!

**10** ★★ **Lies den Dialog zwischen Mrs Walker und ihrer Tochter Helen. Überlege, welche Verben im *simple present* und welche im *present progressive* stehen müssen. Fülle dann die Lücken aus.**

Mrs Walker: "Helen?"

Helen: "Yes, Mum. I ______________________ (be) upstairs in Simon's room."

Mrs Walker: " What ______ you ______________________ (do) there?"

Helen: "I ______________________ (look) for my new CD. Simon often

______________________ (take) my CDs."

Mrs Walker: "But he always ______________________ (give) them back

to you. Why don't you look in the living room first? You usually

______________________ (listen) to your CDs down here."

**11** ★★ **Übersetze.**

a) Es regnet. Warum wäschst du dein Auto?

____________________________________________

b) Ich wasche samstags immer mein Auto.

____________________________________________

c) Die Kinder spielen gerade Monopoly.

____________________________________________

d) Spielen die Kinder oft nachmittags zusammen?

____________________________________________

# Lösungen

## 1 Simple present

**1** a) We live in a small village
b) I usually ride my bike to school
c) They work in the city centre.
d) You speak too fast!
e) I love pizza
f) We often play computer games.
g) Ben and Andy never go shopping.
h) You watch a lot of TV.

**2** a) I am a very big animal.
b) My voice sounds like a trumpet.
c) I live in Africa or in Asia.
d) The colour of my skin is grey.
e) You call my nose a "trunk".
f) I carry heavy things or people on my back.
g) Some of my brothers and sisters work in circuses.
h) Silly people laugh about my ears.
The name of the animal: elephant

**3** a) sing a song
b) go shopping
c) tell the time
d) drink a glass of water
e) ask a question
f) write a letter
g) come here

**4** a) oft
b) immer
c) oft
d) gewöhnlich / normalerweise
e) manchmal
f) nie/niemals
g) manchmal
h) immer
i) selten
j) nie

**5** a) hinter dem Verb
b) vor dem Verb
c) vor dem Verb
d) am Satzanfang

**6** Reihenfolge: d, f, a, g, c, b, e

**7** a) plays, carries, goes, says, tries, buys; does, watches, dies, kisses, has, makes
b) to do, to go, to have, to say (nur in der Aussprache)

**8** a) Jonas comes from Frankfurt.
b) Marie never answers a question.
c) Michael usually watches a film on Saturday evening.
d) Caroline sends a lot of texts.

**9** be have got turn sing go need cut heat put add cook feel

a) is
b) has got
c) turns
d) sings
e) goes
f) needs
g) cuts
h) heats
i) puts
j) adds
k) cooks
l) feels

**10** a) I don't buy expensive clothes.
b) Birds don't sing at night.
c) You don't know my name.
d) We don't watch TV in the evening.
e) I don't enjoy swimming.
f) Lucas and Sophie don't watch videos.

**11** a) Cats don't bark.
b) Dogs don't talk.
c) Frogs don't ride a bike.
d) Birds don't say Good night.
e) A mouse doesn't sing.
f) And budgies don't swim.
g) A hamster doesn't fly.
h) And zebras don't even try.

**12** a) haven't got
b) doesn't know
c) don't find
d) haven't got
e) isn't
f) doesn't look at
g) don't meet
h) doesn't wait

**13** a) isn't / is not
b) doesn't / does not play
c) don't / do not collect
d) hasn't / has not got
e) doesn't / does not go
f) haven't / have not got
g) doesn't / does not draw
h) doesn't / does not like

**14** Paul Kingsley is a famous pop star. He lives in a very big house near London. He has a big swimming pool in his garden and he often invites his friends round for a party. He doesn't walk and he doesn't ride a bike, either. When he goes out, he drives an expensive red sports car. Sometimes he even flies in his private jet!

**15** *Lösungsvorschlag:*
I like parties because my friends are there / the music is often good / because parties are a lot of fun.
I don't like parties because parties are a lot of work / because it's often too noisy there / because parties are very expensive.

**16** a) I am Danny.
b) I am from Sheffield.
c) They are from Sheffield, too.
d) We are new here.
e) And who is that in that photo?
f) That is my sister.

**17** Sorry, I am not Ken, I am Tom. … We aren't from Bristol. We are from York. Are you new here? Yes, we are. Is the girl over there your sister? No, she isn't. She isn't my sister. Is Tanya in your class? No, she isn't in my class. She is in my sister's class. … Are they in your class? No, they aren't in my class either. … He is our teacher. He is our caretaker.

**18** a) Mr and Mrs Benson have got a son.
b) They have got a daughter, too.
c) Mr Benson has got an interesting job.
d) The Bensons have got a house.
e) They have got a car, too.
f) Mrs Benson has got a sister.
g) She has got a nice house in the country.
h) She has got two children, too.

**19** a) The Owens haven't got a flat, they have got a house.
b) Their house has got five rooms.
c) David has got a room and Sheila has got a room, too.
d) Danny hasn't got a big room.
e) Mr and Mrs Owen have got a car.
f) Sheila has got a bike.
g) David has got a bike, too.
h) Danny hasn't got a bike because he is too young.
i) But he has got two big toy cars in his room.

**20** Sam hasn't got a brother, but he's got an aunt.;
Ken hasn't got a sister, but he's got a brother.;
The Bensons haven't got a flat. They've got a house.;
Emma has got a bike. She hasn't got a car.

**21** a) I am Tim. I have got a sister.
b) Suzy is funny. She has got a lot of humour.
c) Sometimes we have got problems and we are angry at each other.
d) School is okay. All of my friends are there, too.

**22** a) You mustn't text and ride your bike. It's too dangerous.
b) She needn't go to bed now. She can go later.
c) I needn't wash my hands. They aren't dirty.
d) Philip mustn't drink milk. He's allergic to it.
e) We mustn't forget our pencils. We need them for the test.

**23** a) must
b) mustn't
c) needn't
d) needn't
e) can't

**24** a) No, you needn't.
b) Yes, you must.
c) No, you needn't.
d) No, you may not.
e) Yes, you must.
f) Yes, you can.
g) Yes, they may, …

**25** a) Shall / ~~Must~~
b) can / ~~mustn't~~
c) must / ~~needn't~~
d) ~~Shall~~ / May
e) must / ~~could~~
f) ~~mustn't~~ / needn't
g) mustn't / ~~must~~
h) ~~shall~~ / could
i) could / ~~may~~
j) ~~can~~ / cannot; can / ~~needn't~~
k) ~~must~~ / can
l) ~~cannot~~ / mustn't

**26** a) needn't / need not
b) mustn't / must not
c) can
d) needn't / need not
e) can
f) mustn't / must not
g) must
h) needn't / need not
i) can
j) can't / cannot

**27** a) *David:* "Mrs Carter, may I have another bowl of soup, please?"
b) *Mrs Carter:* "Yes, of course you may / can."
c) *David:* "There is a party at school today. May I go, please?"
d) *Mrs Carter:* "No, you may not / can't go alone.
e) But you may / can take your friend Justin with you."

**28** a) Tidy
b) go / buy
c) be / be
d) wash
e) be

**29** a) Do not / Don't run around alone.
b) Wait for the group.
c) Do not / Don't feed the animals.
d) Do not / Don't throw anything.

**30** a) Don't forget your homework.
b) Don't talk to your neighbour.
c) Listen to me.
d) Don't be late.
e) Don't do your homework now, do it later.
f) Don't be so loud.

**31** a) Do
b) Does
c) do
d) Does
e) does
f) do

**32** a) Has your brother got a computer? Yes, he has.
b) Have your parents got a new car? No, they haven't. They have still got their old car.
c) Has your teacher got a new baby? No, he hasn't.

**33** a) Yes, he does.
b) No, I don't.
c) No, she doesn't.
d) No, they don't.
e) Yes, she does.

**34** a) Yes, it is.
b) Yes, he is.
c) No, I'm not.
d) Yes, it is.
e) No, it isn't.
f) No, there aren't.
g) No, it isn't.
h) Yes, I am.

**35** a) No, they don't.
b) No, she doesn't.
c) Yes, I do.
d) Yes, it does.
e) No, we don't.

**36** a) Yes, I do.
b) No, she doesn't.
c) Yes, we do.
d) Yes, he does.

**37** a) Is it your birthday party? No, it isn't.
b) Is David's sister at your party? Yes, she is.
c) Are your parents out? Yes, they are.
d) Are there any girls from your class here? Yes, there are.
e) Are you and Sheila in David's class? No, we aren't.

**38** a) Are you from York? Yes, I am.
b) Are your parents from York, too? Yes, they are.
c) Are you often in Fulford? Yes, I am.

**39** *Lösungsvorschläge:*
- Has your mother / your father / your English teacher / your boyfriend got a hamster / a girlfriend / an elephant / a taxi / a dog / a teddy / a football? – Yes, he / she has. / No, he / she hasn't.
- Have you / your parents / your friends got a hamster / a girlfriend / an elephant / a taxi / a dog / a teddy / a football? – Yes, I / they have. / No, I / they haven't.

**40** a) Do you live in London Road?
b) Does John play basketball?
c) Do Alex and Andy eat cheese?

**41** a) Do you want an ice cream?
b) Does Ellie like her teachers?
c) Where does James buy his jeans?
d) When does Mrs Seth do the shopping?
e) Do you watch TV in the morning?
f) When does your first lesson start?
g) Do you have lunch at the school cafeteria?
h) Does Amar want a pet?
i) Do you know a lot of film stars? (auch möglich: Do a lot of film stars know you?)

**42** a) What is the date today? – It's 27th May.
b) How are you? – I'm fine, thanks.
c) Where is your homework? – It's at home. Sorry!
d) Who is in the kitchen? – That's my dad.
e) Where is Felix? – He's in the playground.
f) Who is Felix? – He's a boy in my class.

**43** Subjekt: a) who, b) what
Verb: what
Objekt: a) who, b) what
Ort: where
Zeit: when

**44** b) Who is Mr Braun? He's my German teacher.
c) Where's your classroom? It's upstairs on the left.
d) Who are those boys? They're on the football team.
e) Where are the sandwiches? They're in the kitchen.
f) Who is Luke? He's my cousin.
g) Where are my books? They're in your bag.
h) Who is that girl? I don't know her name.

**45** a) Where do you live?
b) Where do your parents work?
c) When do they get up?
d) When do you get up?
e) When do your lessons begin?

## 2 Present progressive

**1**

| | |
|---|---|
| cleaning | washing |
| singing | laughing |
| talking | fighting |
| drinking | eating |
| listening | shouting |
| knocking | doing |
| watching | fixing |
| going | buying |
| playing | saying |
| crying | trying |
| carrying | looking |

**2**

| | |
|---|---|
| writing | choosing |
| losing | coming |
| riding | taking |
| changing | having |
| driving | tripping |
| planning | putting |
| sitting | clapping |
| running | dropping |
| stopping | swimming |
| cutting | getting |
| forgetting | lying |
| dying | tying |
| slicing | travelling |

**3** a) The sun is shining.
It's not raining.
The birds are singing.
And we are sitting indoors!
We are doing a test.
Look! Mike is dreaming.
He is listening to the birds.
Our teacher is trying to talk to Mike.
b) Die Handlung läuft gerade ab, ist also noch nicht abgeschlossen.

**4** a) The Smiths are spending a weekend at the seaside in Brighton.
b) They are having a lot of fun on the beach.
c) Tim is chasing Suzy in the water.
d) Mrs Smith is buying some ice-cream.
e) Mr Smith is reading a book.
f) A lot of other people are enjoying their time on the beach, too.
g) A little child is building a sand castle.
h) An old man is trying to catch a fish.
i) A girl is drinking a bottle of cold coke.
j) Another girl is drawing a picture of the sea.
k) A woman is sleeping on her sunbed.
l) A boy is looking at a sailing boat.
m) His brother is calling his girl-friend.
n) Some teenagers are playing volleyball.
o) A dog is swimming in the water.

**5** *Next year, then, the next day, every morning, after that, the next evening, seldom* sind keine Signalwörter für das *present progressive*.

**6** a) Bill is getting up now.
b) I am writing a birthday card for Jamie.
c) All the children are dancing.
d) Rosie is feeling tired.
e) We are having a nice time.
f) They are putting their books on the desk.
g) I am listening to a CD.

**7** a) The pupils aren't sitting in their chairs.
b) They are not doing their exercises.
c) They aren't taking notes.
d) They aren't looking at their exercise books.
e) They aren't working.
f) Tom isn't sleeping.
g) Mike isn't flirting with Alice.

**8** a) am not going/ 'm not going
b) are not swimming/aren't swimming
c) are not dancing/aren't dancing
d) are not jumping/aren't jumping
e) is not climbing/isn't climbing
f) are not kicking/aren't kicking
g) is not fighting/isn't fighting

**9** a) Maggie isn't running in the park.
b) We aren't helping our mum.
c) They children aren't answering the questions.
d) You aren't talking about the football match.

**10** b) Jack and Marc are watching TV.
c) Amelie is reading a book.
d) Jack and Marc aren't reading a book.
e) Amelie isn't trying on shoes.
f) Jack and Marc are trying on shoes.
g) Amelie is buying a magazine.
h) Jack and Marc aren't buying a magazine.

**11** a) No, I'm not.
b) No, I'm not.
c) Yes, they are.
d) No, it isn't.
e) No, we aren't.

**12** a) Yes, I am.
b) No, they aren't.
c) No, she / he isn't.
d) No, they aren't.
e) No, I'm not.

**13** a) Yes, he is.
b) No, he isn't.
c) No, they aren't.
d) Yes, she is.
e) No, he isn't.
f) No, they aren't.
g) Yes, he is.
h) Yes, she is.

**14** a) Are you waiting for me? – Yes, I am.
b) Is he looking for his jacket? – No, he isn't.
c) Am I using your pen? – No, you aren't.
d) Are they winning the match? – Yes, they are.
e) Is your dog barking out there? – Yes, it is.
f) Are we finishing the lesson now? – No, we aren't.
g) Is Catherine eating spaghetti? – No, she isn't.

**15** a) Is Tom sitting in his chair?
b) Is he doing an exercise?
c) Are Kevin and Ken making the girls angry?
d) Is Alice flirting with Mike?
e) Is Robert lying on the floor?
f) Are Ben and John playing cards?
g) Is Debbie reading a magazine?
h) Is Fiona running around the classroom?

**16** a) Are they playing the drums?
b) Is she sitting next to her friend Amy?
c) Is Jack showing his parents the classrooms?
d) Is the English teacher dancing with the Maths teacher?

**17** a) Is the cat sitting on the chair?
b) Are the children jumping on the bed?
c) Are we eating fish today?

**18** a) Where are you going?
b) What are you doing?
c) Why are you not listening? / Why aren't you listening?
d) Who is talking?
e) What are you reading?
f) Why are you leaving the room?
g) Why are you not taking notes? / Why aren't you taking notes?
h) Why aren't you doing this exercise? / Why are you not doing this exercise?

**19** a) What was your wife wearing at the party?
b) Who was sitting at your table with you?
c) What were you having for dinner?
d) Why were you laughing so much?

**20** a) Where is this woman reading a book?
b) What is that woman drinking?
c) What is this man buying?
d) Why is that man laughing?

**21** a) What is he doing?
b) What is he doing?
c) Who is drawing a picture?
d) Why is he singing a song?
e) What is he eating?
f) Who is coming upstairs?
g) What is he doing?
h) What is he doing?

**22** b) Where are you going? – To town.
c) What are you eating? – A sandwich.
d) Who are you talking to? – Andy.
e) What are you looking for? – My German book.
f) How are you feeling? – Very happy!
g) What are you doing? – I'm reading a text from Tim.
h) What are you looking at? – A photo of Molly's cat.

**23** a) Who is writing a maths test? Sheila is.
b) Where is her maths book? It's under her desk.
c) Who is she looking at? She's looking at her teacher.
d) Who is he looking at? He is looking at her.

**24** a) What are you looking for?
b) Who are you waiting for?
c) Who are you looking at?
d) What are you listening to?
e) What are you talking about?
f) Who are you looking after?
g) Who are you thinking of?
(think of = denken an; think about = nachdenken über)
h) Why are you running away?
i) What are you writing down?
j) What word are you looking up?
k) What trousers are you trying on?

**25** a) to get off a bus
b) to turn it off
c) to take it off
d) to put them on
e) to wake up

**26** … It's not that her parents do not like pets, but Mrs Owen thinks that she has already got three children and that she doesn't need another baby to look after. … He always runs around and like most small dogs he barks a lot. Can you hear him? He is barking now!

… because not everybody likes to hear him … because he can't understand why his people throw shoes at him when he only wants to warn them against burglars.

## 3 Simple present oder present progressive?

**1** a) We are having a lot of fun at this party.
b) I sometimes travel by plane.
c) "Where are the boys?" "They are swimming in the sea."
d) Are you watching this video?
e) Do you always eat lunch at school?
f) Martin gets up early on Monday mornings.
g) It's late. I am going to bed now.

**2** a) Jonas plays football every Wednesday afternoon.
b) Fiona is playing the guitar in her bedroom.
c) I don't eat eggs because I don't like them.
d) We aren't eating eggs today. We are eating chicken.
e) "What are you doing?" "I am helping my dad in the garden.

**3** a) He lives in London now.
b) I'm watching the football match on TV.
c) They are playing against another school. Do you play football, too?
d) What are you doing there? – I'm very busy. I'm doing my homework.

**4** a) likes
b) is drinking
c) is
d) wants
e) cannot / can't
f) is
g) is trying
h) cannot / can't
i) must
j) has
k) is not / isn't
l) climbs
m) is not / isn't
n) does not / doesn't know
o) is waiting

**5** Today is Kim's birthday. All her friends want to come to her party. So Kim and her family are very busy. At the moment Kim and her sister, Annabel, are decorating the living room. Kim likes colourful balloons and candles. Her father is buying juice, food and sweets at the supermarket. Her mum is making sandwiches in the kitchen. Kim feels happy. She thinks that everything is great.

**6** a) It is Saturday morning and Tim is cleaning his room at the moment. He usually plays with his friends on Saturdays but today he is staying at home because his mother is angry with him.
b) Mr and Mrs Weaver like action films. So they often go to the cinema together. But today they are watching an exciting film on TV.
c) On Monday afternoons Sam and Kevin often play tennis. But today Kevin is studying for a test and Sam is shopping with his sister, Carol. Sam needs new shoes and Carol knows a lot of good shops.
d) Peter: "Look! That cat over there wants to take a bath in the pond."
Mick: "No, cats hate water. This cat is trying to catch a fish."
Peter: "Oh, you are (oder: you're) right."

**7** a) Mrs Owen works at the Tourist Information Centre.
b) She helps tourists.
c) Sometimes she helps them find a hotel.
d) She answers their questions.
e) She gives them all kind of information about York.
f) Today she is there again.
g) A lot of people are waiting for her.
h) They want to ask her a lot of questions.
i) A tourist is asking her for the way to the station.

**8** a) ✓
b) The children are taking a test this morning.
c) ✓
d) Look, Daniel is wearing his new jacket.

**9** *Lucy:* Oh, hi, Mia. Are you waiting for the Number 3 bus, too?
*Mia:* Hi, Lucy, yes, I am. Where are you going?
*Lucy:* I am going to town.
*Mia:* Me too! I often buy something on Saturdays because my mum gives me money at the weekend.
*Lucy:* That's nice. Oh, look! The bus is coming.

**10** Mrs Walker: "Helen?"
Helen: "Yes, Mum. I am (oder: 'm) upstairs in Simon's room."
Mrs Walker: "What are you doing there?"
Helen: "I am (oder: 'm) looking for my new CD. Simon often takes my CDs."
Mrs Walker: "But he always gives them back to you. Why don't you look in the living room first? You usually listen to your CDs down here."

**11** a) It is raining. Why are you washing (oder: cleaning) your car?
b) I always wash (oder: clean) my car on Saturdays.
c) The children are playing Monopoly.
d) Do the children often play together in the afternoon?

# Besser werden mit dem täglichen 10-Minuten-Training!

- Kleine Lernportionen: In 10 Minuten das Wichtigste draufhaben
- Mit vielen Übungen zu einem Schlüsselthema
- Mit leichten und schweren Übungen für mehr Lernerfolg

ISBN 978-3-12-927386-9

ISBN 978-3-12-927387-6

ISBN 978-3-12-927388-3

ISBN 978-3-12-927389-0

ISBN 978-3-12-927392-0

ISBN 978-3-12-927393-7

ISBN 978-3-12-927394-4

ISBN 978-3-12-927395-1

ISBN 978-3-12-927396-8

Diese und weitere Lernhilfen sind im Buchhandel erhältlich.
Weitere Informationen unter **www.klett-lerntraining.de**